# From DISGRACE to GRACE

WILLIAM L. BROWNING

ISBN 979-8-89243-680-9 (paperback)
ISBN 979-8-89243-681-6 (digital)



Christian Faith Publishing
832 Park Avenue
Meadville, PA 16335
www.christianfaithpublishing.com

Printed in the United States of America

# Acknowledgments

When *God* wants us to accomplish something, *He* always provides a way for us to complete what *He* needs done. I was able to provide my story, and *God* sent my niece, Lisa, to help me put it on paper.

My wife, Diane, helped in bringing to the front of my mind the awesome things *God* has allowed us to experience.

# Introduction

As I write this, I am led by the Holy Spirit by giving me a continued, steady flow of thoughts. I get extremely excited to be used by God, and I can take no credit or claim that I have ever done anything right. It is like I am talking or writing what He tells me, and I am truly blessed by God letting me be His secretary. I know this book was given to me by God because some of this I do not remember. I know why He did it, so there would be no mistakes if I meditated on *His* word and allowed *Him* to work through me. This book is dedicated to my wife, Diane, and my children and grandchildren

I ask God to humble me. I need *His* anointing to do *His* will. *God* says, "I've given you my anointing. You don't have an anointing. Its mine. You're like an ink pen." Second Corinthians, chapter 3, verse 3, talks about the pen. I thought I was losing my ministry. He said, "Teach what I did, not what You did, because you did nothing. You are only getting a look at what I was doing. I have the glory. I have placed it in you. It's like an ink pen. I filled it up. And as I need it, it comes out. I'll tell you where to go. I'll tell you what to say. I'll send people to you that I want you to minister to. You speak, and I'll do the work. They need to be healed. I will heal them through you."

He also is pleased and enjoying what I am doing.

"You forgot what I sent you, for I sent you up to Canada to touch people. You can use your testimony with what I've done in your life to bring people to Me. I'm no longer sending you back to Canada to preach but to teach and give your testimony of what I have done."

That's what I wanted to do. *He* uses me to touch, to speak. He does all things. I do nothing. According to Psalm 105, it says to speak of all *God's* works, work of His hands and *His* miracles *He* performs. I wondered why I was not going back to Canada. But then I realized, COVID was used to restrict the borders. I can't go back across until it's time to go back. God says, "You want to, but you're not qualified right now." I needed the patience to do what God wanted me to do.

"Be patient. I'll fill you up, and then I will send you back."

# Chapter 1

I was born on August 21,1944, in Allen Junction, West Virginia. I attended a small church in Madeline Holler off and on until the age of ten. At the age of ten, my family moved to Oregon, where my parents worked in the fields, picking apples. It was seasonal work for the summer. And at the end of fall, we moved to Walla Walla, Washington, where my father worked, harvesting wheat and running a combine the following summer. My family returned to West Virginia when I turned twelve, and my father resumed work in the coal mines for a year. My father was diagnosed with black lung and retired from coal mining. My father purchased a farm in Keavy, Kentucky. He continued to work jobs such as logging timber and providing most of our needs by farming the land and selling produce. During my years of adolescence, he became a Christian and helped to build a small church in Madeline Holler. He would travel within Madeline, West Virginia. And while there, he would help in building the church.

Once the church was built, we had a few Black families who joined the church, but they were to be seated at the back of the church. This caused me to become confused because my family had Black friends and friends that were hobos. They rode freight trains near our home, and my mother would make meals we would eat with them. I did not understand why they were welcome in our home, yet at church they were segregated and placed in the back of the church. The Church of Christ that we attended in Kentucky played music. We also would visit another Church of Christ that did not allow music. The difference in doctrines between the two churches was confusing to me because I thought churches had all the same beliefs. I wondered why one church had music and singing and another would only sing with no instruments. I was also confused about the separation of races.

In high school, I joined the football team. I thought football would allow me to feel included. In the evenings, I would help my father work on the farm. I was injured playing football. My knee was torn. My coach took me to the doctors at school, and then he took me home. My father did not seem concerned about my knee, only that I was unable to work in the farm. The day after my injury, I returned to school, and a girl named Shirley stole my football jacket. She refused to give it back until I kissed her. I was embarrassed, so I gave her a quick peck on the cheek.

I was not allowed to date. My dad said I would get myself into trouble. I became very insecure and thought no one would be my friend because I had been told I was stupid and would never amount to anything.

We lived in a lot of various places; we were never in one place for exceedingly long. I had no social skills and did not have many friends. I had a fear of never being in one place too long and did not have many friends because of my early years of living in different states with no permanent home life and virtually no social life. I started to feel inferior and insecure. This had a huge effect on my self-esteem with little positive influence or positive statements about me. This led to social problems as I grew older. I was becoming more competent. I came to realize my parents loved me, but because of their upbringing, they did not know how to give me positive encouragement. Their lives and upbringing were a factor in the way they raised me.

My parents grew up in very tough times. They had also moved a lot as children. There was a lot of abuse physically, emotionally, and sexually, especially in my mother's young childhood. I understood later in my life how my parents' childhoods affected them and how they raised me. My father was on his own from the age of twelve, and my mother was on her own from the age of fourteen. My father was born on January 20, 1901. My mother was born on February 28, 1902. They were married on July 21, 1921. They had three children at the time of the Great Depression. Life had always been hard for my parents. I was told by my siblings, because I was the youngest of five children, that my parents had struggled with alcohol. I remember seeing my dad's hands bleeding from the cold and demanding work. Mom would do without food sometimes and sacrificed a lot so her children would have enough to eat and be presentable for school. When my father was unable to work, my mother would do odd jobs and take care of the farm. To ensure I always had what I needed, they raised me away from the worldly atmosphere of alcohol and sin as much as possible. They showed their love by sacrificing for us.

I realized they did the best for me that they had been equipped with. My parents showed love in ways I could not appreciate until I left home. My mom and dad had surrendered their life to the Lord. It changed their life for the better, and they were able to show love.

After graduation, I left home and moved to Markesan, Wisconsin and worked in a vegetable-packing plant. While in Wisconsin, at the age of seventeen, I befriended a young lady, who worked with me, by the name of Patricia. She was my first experience in dating. This relationship was purely platonic, and she became my first faithful friend. I returned home to my parents for a week, then traveled to Florida, where I picked fruit for about two weeks. I then tired of picking fruit and took a job working on a boat dock in Tampa for about a month. I then moved to Big Lake, Texas, and worked setting up charges for explosions to be registered on a seismograph. The vibrations located the oil underground. After approximately six months, I decided to move to my sister's home in Bud, West Virginia. My sister had sent me money for a bus ticket home. I worked stocking produce to repay my bus ticket for about two weeks. At the age of eighteen, I joined the Air Force at the Beckley, West Virginia office. I enlisted for four years, and basic training was six weeks long. This consisted of disciplined training and how to obey orders and survive. Then I attended tech school for sixteen weeks (about three and a half months), learning how to become a mechanic, working on jet engines and aircraft. After tech school, I visited my parents for a few days. I then flew to Chicago to visit an old friend. It was nice to see Patricia, and I thought, what a nice and honest person Pat had turned out to be.

My first station was on the island of Okinawa. This is when I started drinking and partying. The drinking began to take over my life. I was drinking in the morning at work and in bars in the evening. I had eventually become a good drinking partner with two World War II sergeants. I realized I did not have the drinking experience to keep up with these two veterans. After approximately eighteen months (about one and a half years), I walked outside and observed acres of lawn covered with thousands of men wearing green uniforms. I asked my friend, "Who are they, and where are they going?"

He replied, "They are going to a place called Vietnam."

I asked, "Where is that?"

He said it was like Hawaii, same weather. I was impressed. I was shipped back to the states to an Air Force base near Fort Bragg, North Carolina. As I was unpacking, I was told I was going back to Okinawa to help set up my job. I remembered Vietnam and asked if I could go there. I put in a request, knowing I would not get it because it was like Hawaii, or so I thought. I was ignorant and should have studied geography more. I returned to Okinawa for thirty days (about four and a half weeks), set up my job, and found out my transfer was granted. When I arrived in Vietnam, I found out the weather was the only thing like Hawaii.

I was given my orders for work to repair and rebuild gas turbine compressors for starting jet engines. After about a month, I met a guy named Hap. This was his nickname. Hap and I rented a house together. He became my best friend. Hap was a large, Black man who took no abuse from anyone. I always felt accepted while around him. He had a caring and loving heart. I asked Hap how he got that nickname. He said it was the initials of his name, and he laughed and said, "Quote, I am Italian and the best Black wop in the Air Force." I started to care for him as a brother. Around May of 1966, I was sent to the Philippines on temporary duty. I had a resentment because everyone else was sent to Australia or Hawaii for thirty days (about four and a half weeks). R 'n' R, I was sent to the Philippines—me and the other eleven people who were sent to Angeles City in the Philippines. We were in Angeles for about seventeen days (about two and a half weeks), drunk, living in bars and sleeping on the side of an open sewer.

We were taken to jail. But upon finding out we were military, they returned us to Clark Air Base and left us there. We went to walk back on base. None of us had showered or shaved for seventeen days (about two and a half weeks). The guard said US civilians were not allowed on base. We explained we were Air Force. We produced our Air Force IDs. And he spoke, "I was waiting for you, and we have a special ride for you guys to your place." We were all put in the stockade. And the next morning, we were sent to the commander's office. We were given a choice for being AWOL: court-martial or an Article 15. We all signed the Article 15. It was a lower level than court-martial, admitting guilt without a trial. The base commander had a rule: If anyone was in trouble on his base for an Article 15, you would be gone before sundown. After signing Article 15, we lost all rank, and our stripes were taken. We were ranked at the lowest ranking of E1. We were now at the airport, being sent back to Vietnam. They were bumping lieutenants, majors, and master sergeants to make sure we were on that flight. Someone asked, "Who are they?" We were taking seats from higher ranked officials. The passengers wondered why we had dark patches instead of stripes. They said we looked more like the dirty dozen, only with eleven instead of twelve. When we got back to Benoit, it took a little while before we got our rank back. Later, December 16, about ten or eleven, I was given a ride back to base. A little while later, we were out drinking. And in an alley, we started coming under a mortar attack, and the Vietcong had beaten me. I had lost consciousness, and I remembered what I thought was a weird dream and saw colors. There were two beings that I later realized as being angels. I started thinking, *What a weird dream this is.*

The angel on my right said, "This is not a dream." I started to think if this was not a dream, and the same angels said, "We are here to take you to where you are going." They left. And after a long time, I heard a voice saying, "Take him back. I am not finished with him yet." The second time, the voice said it again. It was like going through light, and I remember waking up, and it was on the back of a helicopter. The medic cursed and said, "Lie down. You will get us all killed." I remember explosions and woke up in 3rd Field Hospital in Ho Chi Minh City three days later. I was transferred to Wright-Patterson Hospital, where I stayed till August. I reenlisted for four more years. Some of us never learned.

As I drank, I started to feel guilt from Vietnam. And one night, I went to the NCO desk and went to the stag bar to be alone. An old chief master asked me, "Were you in Vietnam?" I said yes, and he said they would not let him go and started to argue and told the bartender to give me a beer. I replied, "Do not drink beer."

He pointed to all his stripes and said, "Give him two beers." I said okay, and I downed them. Then I told the bartender to give my friend two whiskeys, and he said, "I do not drink whiskey."

I told him, "You can drink them or wear them."

The bartender said, "Please do not make him drink," then I said okay, and I took them off the canteen and threw them on him and left and went back to the barracks. But I forgot I lived in town. I destroyed a lot, and eight MPs finally got me to the stockade. In the morning, the first sergeant came in and took me out and asked, "Why? You have a perfect record." I saw the barracks room I had destroyed and blood on the walls and thought, *I am done.*

I was assigned to cut flowers around the orderly room, and I was on separate rations and had no money to buy food. There was a nice redheaded lieutenant who would go to lunch and knew I was hungry and bought me a meal. Then I was put back into the barracks for the rest of my time. I was escorted to the commander's office and asked, "What do you want?"

I responded with, "I am done, and I am getting out."

The colonel said, "Do not come into my office and tell me what you are going to do."

The first sergeant said, "Sir, he has had enough and wants to be reassigned."

The colonel said, "Well, get him an appointment with the chaplain and a psychiatrist."

I saw the chaplain, and he sent me to see the psychiatrist. I went in, and he said, "I will be back." About fifteen minutes later, he came back. "You need a discharge. You have not talked to me," he said. I know enough. I was ignorant that the colonel had already said okay. I left Fort Bragg and came to Flint, Michigan, and applied for a job at GM.

## Angel experience

One morning leaving work, I started home. And I usually go west, on Route 69. But that morning, for some reason, when under the overpass, I just turned it down Route 23. I saw a man on their side of the road. He had a red bag in his hand. I never pick up hitchhikers. But that morning, for some reason, I stopped and asked him if he needed a ride. He got into the car and said, "You didn't pick me up because you wanted to. You picked me up because God told you to. He wanted me to talk to you." Then I realized I picked up some kind of a nutcase. But he put his red bag in the back seat. Guardian. As we traveled down 23, going south, he started to tell me that he had been to Port Huron, taking another couple over there. And he said that God told him to come back to where he was. And I knew he was out of it.

As we went south on 23, he started to tell me things that no one knew. He started telling me what I would be doing. And I wondered how he knew what I would be doing. As we proceeded south, we passed the road I usually exit to go home. And I don't know why, but I kept going Hatra while we came to the Silver Lake Road. And I told him, "I have to let you off here because my house is back the other way." So he got out and started to take his bag out. I asked him if he needed some money. He said, "No, I don't need any money."

I knew then he was different. He had told me he would like to go somewhere for coffee. So I explained to him, "I think God wants me to give you this coffee and money to help you out." So he said okay. We had been talking about God. And as I pulled out and remembered we had a church meeting that night on Saturday, I thought I should have invited him with me. So I stopped and backed up to talk to him, but he was gone. No cars around. And I knew then, he had to be an angel. I looked back. I think I've had encountered with angels before. As a matter of fact, I know, when I was in Moosonee in Canada, I had an encounter.

*****

I knew I would not get a job because of my looks, being dirty and disheveled. The interviewer asked how long I served. I told him. And he asked, "What time do you get up?"

I said, "I will be here at 5:00 a.m.

He said, "You are hired."

While I was in Vietnam, I saw so many ungodly things. I started to trade whiskey for opium and thought, *This is a good deal. It is better than drinking.* I thought there could not be a God. After I started work at GM, I was a loner. I stayed away from people. And when around them, I tried to be nice to them if I wanted something from them. I found out who the drug dealers were and became their best customers. And after ninety days (about three months), I was a permanent employee. I did not have to worry because I was a union member. I found out how to play the game of corruption, stealing, cheating, lies, and evil.

I was learning to use the system to my advantage. I had mental problems and guilt from past things. I would stay high or drink most of the time. We would go back and sit among the crates to hide from the supervisors and do drugs we knew nothing about. One day, one of the groups brought some pot, but it was laced with something strong. When I went home, I did not come back for a few days. The drugs took a while to get out of my system. I was paranoid and afraid to leave the house. As far as I knew, it was laced with acid or heroin. I was on a downward spiral with alcohol, drugs, and bad decisions.

New Year's Day 1975, I went to Kmart to buy my daughter a birthday present and was sitting in my van. Some guy came up and handed me a magazine about an organized political party. I found out later, it was a communist group. After giving me the magazine, he wanted it back. I told him it was mine and he could not get it back. As I raised my arms to let him get it, I was angry because he had been talking about veterans in a very degrading way. I was so mad when he reached for his paper. I used my hands to jam him in the steering wheel and fell out on top of him in the snowbank, and the police were called. As we got into the car, I was told I was the cause of the fight, and the next time, if I got into a fight with one of the groups, I had to better make sure they were really hurt because they had given the police hell and harassed people all through the holiday.

# Chapter 2

I had taken Moonman home with me to meet my wife. When he left, she said, "Why don't you find a few friends who do not look so cruddy with that long hair?"

I told her, "You do not complain about my long hair hanging down to my waist."

After a month or so, I came home and found them sitting at the table laughing, and I thought maybe they had an affair as he must have been nice around her. She got up and said, "I must go fold clothes or something." So Moon told me, "Your wife thinks you have a drug or alcohol problem." She asked if he would talk to me. I thought she was the one who had the drug problem. *Who does she think he is that he could help me?* But I said, "Okay, I will call and make an appointment."

He said, "It is already done. I have one for you today."

I said, "I must work today."

He said, "He is just an old gullible man, and he will write you an excuse. So you will not have to worry."

I got excited to get a note, saying I was excused. We made plans to see the old man he had said was gullible and would believe anything he said. Moon said he was a good friend, and I knew the old man was not very smart to have one nasty-looking hippie for a friend. After a while, some lady said he was ready to see me. I walked in, and he was lying back in his chair, feet on the table with a stupid grin. He said, "I hear you are an alcoholic." I said no. He said, "I hear you like to get high." He asked if I did not drink, what do I use? I told him I use meth, heroin mixed with pot, and cocaine. His response was, "I guess you do not have a problem with getting high. I see from what you said, you are not only an alcoholic, but you are also a drug addict. Since I cannot help you, you need to leave."

I got angry and said, "I do not need any help" as I reached for the door.

He said, "Hey, I looked at him." He laughed and said, "You will be back."

I thought, *You old coot.*

When Moon saw me, he smiled and said, "Did the old man convince you that you have a problem?" I said no. Moon said, "I can" and pulled out his wallet, took out a piece of paper, and asked, "Whose name is that?"

I said, "Mine."

Then he opened the rest of the paper and started to read date and time, type of drug, and the amount and quantity. He then said to me, "You are facing five counts of delivery each, seven years. That's thirty-five years. But you have a nice wife and three children. So the dumb old man and I agree. You have two choices: thirty-five years or see the man until you are cured."

So I thought, *A couple of years, and I will be fine.* I agreed and set an appointment to see him. I opened the door to John's office, and he was still at the same desk, same way. And he said with a big smile, "I told you, you would be back." I did not respond because *I was annoyed.*

After a few months, I began to enjoy seeing him. I went to human sensitivity and sexuality classes. I also went back to college and studied to be a premedical student. After about one or two years, my wife called me and said to meet John on Detroit Street after work. He wanted me to work for him. I thought as a janitor or cleaner in the evenings. I asked him what he wanted, and he said, "I could use you as a counselor."

My reply was, "Do not know if I am qualified."

John said, "You went to my classes. And if you weren't qualified, you would not get the job."

I said, "Okay." I had to go until I remained sober. I attended my first meeting. It was in Flint, Michigan, at the Arid Club. I was supposed to go to the third floor. I looked for a meeting because John said, "I need to know if you attended or not." I could not figure out how he would know. I walked past one of the rooms. I saw some men in business suits as I walked past one of them, and one of them said, "Hey, who are you looking for?"

I said, "The AA meeting."

He said, "It is in here. And I knew you were coming." Then I wondered, how did they know I was coming? I found out, the men in business suits were friends of John Cranes.

I started going to meetings and was a little surprised I found myself enjoying them. I met the old men that knew a lot more than I did. Lenny, aka moon, became my friend and helped me to recover from alcoholism. My thinking had changed from my past experiences during this time. I was a confessed atheist. I had joined my friend Lenny at his job. I did not find out until later that he was working with the ATF. So, as I was attending AA meetings, step three was to become willing to turn our life over to God. I was confused, said I would, but there was no change in my actions. I was still full of anger, guilt, hate, and unforgiveness.

I continued my meetings as part of my punishment or, truly, my agreement to stay out of prison. I had a job with Lenny, working vice. I was going to college, sitting outside the cafeteria, smoking a joint. A man walked up and asked if I was Larry. I said yes. He gave me a card and asked if I wanted to call him. We would work out a deal. I could sign up for his course in criminal justice and help him at work. I could acquire firsthand experience and use that for part of class credit. I inquired as to what the work was. He said special ops. And I asked, "What is that?" He said vice squad. I tried to hide my joint. He smiled and said, "Hope I see you around."

I told Moon I did not like the plan, and he said, "Okay, if you want to change and take the other choice, you can."

I said, "I guess I can do it, so I can stay free."

One time during work with Moon, we stopped at a party store with a group of long-haired hippies standing outside. Police pulled up next to us, and he let his long hair hang out the window of his car. He yelled "pigs" two or three times. I thought we would go to jail, but the police officer just yelled, "Stupid hippie." The guys took off around the corner until the police left. We then walked back out. I told Moon, which was his street name, "Hey, you are bold to yell at the police officers like you did." He told them a story about being caught with drugs. And because of the way he got out of the charges, the police were afraid of him. Then he started to buy drugs from the group of men. He got their phone numbers and the names of their dealers. Later, we busted all of them.

I was continuing with my AA program and started having some thoughts that if *God* did not want me here, He would provide a way for me to attend a Christian-based program. If he genuinely wanted me, and he existed, I would be free from alcohol and drugs. Little did I know, *God* had already started doing a work in me. I had just not been willing to surrender. During my time in AA, I would talk to some of the older men. They would say, "Come here, boy, let us teach you something." I thought they were hillbillies and stupid. The more I went, the more I learned. There were a lot of professionals in AA and, thankfully, a lot of regular folks with only plain common sense. Today AA has changed a little. The old-timers still use the Bible to have meetings. Today we also have the big book.

The third step was to ask for forgiveness and surrender everything to God. I used to talk to people who did not know they had been born again, and I would tell them that God was giving them a clean start.

Some AA members have started to fellowship at church and have started home fellowships. My wife, Diane, and I started a home fellowship, and it grew to forty-two or more. Diane was becoming a little wary with the home fellowship. She said, "They come at nine in the morning, and they stay till 6:00 p.m."

I said, "Yes, it is exciting."

She replied, "I need a break from helping to prepare food and cleaning. It is much different today than it was when Jesus was alive."

Sometimes I wonder why we have changed from that era. We now have all large or superchurches, and for some people, it is harder to fit into large groups. I believe the churches have lost the real love of Christ and are seeking things of the world and have stopped seeking the presence of God. We need to get back to basics and stop going after or looking for answers and love in the wrong place. Church, in some instances, has blinded people's eyes from the truth. For example, some people are taught that AA is not spiritual, which is not true. Some churches will not allow AA to use their churches for meetings. I was told once by a pastor, "We do not want that kind of people here, and I hoped no one believed that." I have experienced it myself though. Now AA is starting to have home fellowships that are enabling AA members to have a place to go. They are truly seeking God. Some AA members have left the church because of hearing the wrong message. They have been hurt and have seen hate in churches. They want more, so I study the Bible and consider these people to be the dry bones talked about in the book of Ezekiel.

In Second Chronicles, you see the church is being split. And I may be wrong, but as I pray, my belief is, it is talking about dry bones, people that have been hurt, rejected, and not felt included because of their past. The day I accepted Jesus, and I felt the love of God. It scared me because I had never experienced true love like that, and I had remembered it was so strong. I was trembling and thought I could not express it. I cried all the way home and started to have people I hated come into my thoughts. My feelings were changing from hatred to love.

One day, after church, I walked into the house and had been weeping from earlier. I had asked my wife, Diane, if she was still paying tithes, and she said, "Only on my money." I told her I wanted her to start paying on mine also. She said, "I do not know what happened, but I remember when I asked God, if He would forgive me, I would surrender everything anytime, total surrender to Him. And I have."

# Chapter 3

Earlier in the week, I had stopped to get a checkup. And as the doctor checked me, there was an air of fear as he left the room. He came back in and said he had an appointment for me at a doctor's office in Flint. I got to the doctor's office. I was given an exam and an appointment for surgery for a biopsy. After the biopsy, I was told it was cancer. I was put on a special diet for twenty-one days (about three weeks), and the doctor said I would be sent to Beaumont Hospital. I was given another surgery to take the lump out. When I came home from surgery, my wife asked me, "Did you talk to the doctor?" I was still drugged up, and I said yes. She said, "You need to call him back. So I did. And he said, "I am sorry, but you are full of cancer, and it has spread. And that is why we are sending you back down to Beaumont Hospital in twenty-one days" (about three weeks). I was not worried because the Lord gave me peace. I had not yet completely given myself over to the Lord. And later, my wife informed me that our daughter, Heather, had been attending church. She believes that God still heals. I said, "Okay, we need to start going to church," and that one sounded good. So we went. And the pastor, I had found out later, had come to my room every day and prayed for me.

We continued to go to church. And later the pastor had asked if I would come up front, and he would anoint me. So, as I was making my way to the altar, I saw a husband and wife walking up with oil. I was a little set back to see the woman because in the churches I had been raised in, women were to remain silent and not to speak or minister. I did not care, though, that she was a female. I knew it would help me with my surgery and results.

I was placed on a special diet for twenty-one days. I would forget where I was, but I had a cell phone and would call my wife, Diane, to get me. She was worried and had stopped letting me drive for a while. I would go to the store for something and ended up in a town I did not know and come home with something else.

We had returned to the hospital. I went in and got a shot of radiation. I was to return at two o'clock that afternoon. When I returned, I was put on a bed, and they checked my neck. The doctor came in and looked at us. He told us he wanted to x-ray my neck and chest. I got up and let him look. Then I started to think it must have spread, and he came out and said, "Go into my office, and I will explain or try to explain what we found." We went into his office, and he showed us the film from Flint and pointed to the spots he had found. He showed us the X-ray he had taken after my surgery. He said, "There is no cancer. I cannot explain it." Being a new theologian, I remembered what the couple said, that I was healed by his stripes.

I was going back every year for ten years. The last time, he said to make sure I needed to get another scan in Flint. I followed his instructions and had the ultrasound done. I went for lunch. And when I arrived at home, my phone was blinking. I answered. The message was noticeably clear, and it made me feel good I was free of cancer. I knew he was one of the best cancer doctors around. I think *God* had sent him here because he wanted me to have the best doctor. I was healed because of my belief in *God* and His ability to free me from cancer. My family doctor was a Christian, He mentored to me and told me, "Larry, I can find the best meds for you, but they only heal if *God* does it." Medicines are only given to you to help; *God* does the healing.

I was very blessed to have the Lord put the best disciples in my life. First, He put a man in my life before I even became a Christian to help start me off. He showed me by example what a Christian was supposed to be. Sometimes *God* used him to stir my spirit and help show me things I needed to know. The first time I went to church at New Life, I saw the pastor, and he came over and said it was nice to see me and was very happy to have me there.

As I started to attend church there, *God* put me there to teach me about love. He placed people in my way to teach me about true love by experience. My friend Terry helped me by allowing me to collaborate with him in the youth group. He was instructing a group. *God* had given him to run, called the gap. I asked him why he called it the gap; he said *God* needed to have a place to fill in the gap between the world and *God*. I started to be included, and it felt good to have someone who wanted to include me in their ministry. I became excited to go and help him with the ministry, and I started to feel the anointing as my wife, Diane, was helping me to change.

My wife, Diane, is *God*'s gift to me. When I met her, she was going to church. She was very spiritual and had a love that was from *God*. I am not saying she was perfect because she made mistakes. I wanted to show her I was a real man and thought it was true, but I knew that Satan had put that thought in my head. I had a lot of guilt because of the evil things in my life. *God*'s love is what made me like her, but I never had love for anyone until I knew Jesus. I knew the Lord put us together because He changed things by giving me the love to keep us together. When you have been kept from women or girls, like my father did with me, growing up, you do not understand that women's thinking is different from men. *God* has taken the feeling of lust from me. When we dated, I did things that I knew she would leave me for, like very evil things. I was so full of drugs and hate. When *God* gives you a free will and you use drugs, it makes you guilty. I knew she loved me, and she was not normal because she lived in the spiritual world that she stayed in consistently. The Bible says we are a peculiar people set apart for *God*, a royal priesthood—peculiar people set apart. Well, I must give *God* all the credit because He gave her a perfect love first. In the book of John, it says, "Perfect love casts out all fear." ("Perfect love uplifts the community" [*New Pittsburgh Courier*].) ("Perfect love uplifts the community" [*New Pittsburgh Courier*].)

While we were dating, I lived on the bad side of Flint. I was so angry one night; I kicked her out in the streets without a car. She got a ride from a friend, but I wondered why she came back. When I overdosed on drugs, she was caring for the children and kept me in prayer. I needed it. I really needed it. One night, when her brother came over with some buckeyes that's chocolate peanut butter candy with a special ingredient, we gave it to her and laughed. She got sick and went to bed, and we thought it was funny, but I still felt guilty about it. So you can read the rest of it about her that I write in the book, but you can see how spiritual she is. It is hard to stop talking about her because I am proof of her commitment to the Lord and how spiritual she is. *God* put her in my life, and she is extraordinarily strong in the Lord.

Diane was an interpreter for the deaf and was asked if she would sign a song. She agreed. So, in a week or two, she would be ready to sign the songs. It gave her time to ask Ken and Judy to help her to sign in American sign language. As Judy would help her, she was getting involved with the children and was gifted to collaborate with them, and I was asked to help her to sign. The night we signed, I told her to pick a spot on the wall and concentrate on that spot. She was extremely nervous to look at the people. As they brought the bus full of kids from Flint to Grand Blanc to church, it started to fill up. One of the guys stood in front of the spot she was looking at and blocked her view. I had told her to just find another spot to look at. As she started to sign, the anointing started to fall, and I started to weep and lost it. The Holy Spirit helped me to finish the song. As soon as I finished, I took off to a room without windows. I did not want to let people see me weeping. It just so happened I went into a room that was full of people. They had the lights off. They were crying, and I really broke down. I did not understand how the Holy Spirit would touch so many people at the same time. Since I have become born again, *I have not had a desire to drink or use drugs*

I had signed or rather helped sign the song before and found out signing has a way of ushering in the Holy Spirit and the anointing. After we had finished signing, Terry spoke and invited the youth to accept Christ. Almost all came up and prayed and invited Jesus into their hearts. After that, I started to get involved and allowed the Holy Spirit to teach me about love and His ways.

As time went on, I really got excited. I had brought in a coffee pot in our work area to help out with the money to use for the gap and some for vacation to Florida. As I started to sell coffee, it started to grow, and I would watch people sit and drink coffee, read magazines. After a while, I realized they were my old *Playboy*s and dirty magazines. I did not think it was right to let them read them. So, as embarrassed as I was, I removed the magazines. I had started to get convicted and decided to get rid of them. I went to work early one morning and got a fifty-five-gallon barre, filled it up and dumped the magazines in the bin outback. I was so ignorant. I left a few for the sinners to look at. God convicted me and spoke, "They all have to go." I couldn't believe I was so ignorant. God also used those experiences to teach me not to judge young Christians because some of them are ignorant also.

## Saginaw ministries

Upon returning home, I returned to my ministry in Saginaw. As I was teaching about the anointing, a young man came up and asked me to pray for him to receive the anointing. I asked him, "Why do you want to receive the anointing?"

He said, "I'm going back to the streets to preach."

So I laid hands on him, and the glory was so strong. He fell, and he started weeping. The next man came up, and I ask him, "What do you want?"

He said, "I want the anointing and my foot healed."

I said, "Okay, what you ask for tonight, God's going to give you." Then I looked down and said, "Oh, Lord, forgive me. I don't have the faith to pray for his foot." I started praying, but I didn't know what to do. So I said to the little guy that I just prayed for, "God wants you to pray for the man's foot." He was crying while he prayed for the man's foot. The man's foot began to move and straightened. He started to cry, and he said, "Is that okay?"

I was crying and said, "Yeah."

Another young man came up and asked me if I could go pray for Joe. He said, "Joe has cancer and has maybe thirty days to live."

So I told him, "Okay."

We went back to Joe, and I asked him, "Do you believe God heals?" He said yes. So I asked him, "Would you help me to pray?" He said okay. Joe, after a while, got up and began to run around the room. The guys were afraid he would hurt himself. I told them, "Don't be afraid. He's healed." I went back a year later, and Joe was there again. Then I was amazed to see he had been truly healed. After the meeting, I went home, and each time we went back to the rescue mission, we would see things happening. My wife and I ministered with the ladies; they were being filled with the Holy Spirit. We saw miracles and signs and wonders.

*****

Terry started taking us camping on the river up north with a group from the church. It led to the youth going with us. We would sing at night, and a lot of the campers would come over and watch us. It began to be an annual event and grow. One night, we took our worship team as part of it up with us, and so we were singing. One night, we had our grandson Nick with us, and after a few songs, Jim offered to take requests. My grandson said, "Hey, how about 'Trashy Women.'"

Jim smiled and said, "Okay," with a silly grin and played part of it, and the church clapped and said, "Thanks, Nick," which made him feel included.

Understanding goes a long way, but a religious spirit drives a wedge between *us* and the world. So I thank God for Jim and our church.

One weekend, we went camping. As we were leaving, I saw Terry with a silly grin, and I waited to see what he was up to. He was just smiling. So we went home after a great weekend. As I was unpacking our trailer, I found a bag of chicken bones that some of the guys and Terry put in my trailer to honor me by letting me dump them. Well, Terry was so curious. He called me to see if I found them, and I said yes. But when he asked, "Are you upset?"

I said, "No. But my dog found them and choked and died, but that is okay."

When he heard that, he started to say, "I am so sorry," and I knew he was really feeling guilty.

So I laughed and said, "It is okay, but I thought two can play the same game. It is nice to have fun with friends, and I thought you can help me learn about God. But God started to give me a sense of humor."

We started making money from our coffee pot. But after I had gotten rid of my rotten magazines, our business started to take a loss. Then we decided to take the money we got to buy pizzas for the youth at the gap, and it got around that we were helping the youth at church. Later, when word got out, we began to grow our business. We were having a hard time keeping up with sales because it was known the money was used for the youth.

I wanted to help the young people to realize how blessed they are, so I asked God to open doors for me. He had done this with Terry and the youth group.

I was beginning to read the Bible and seek for knowledge from the Holy Spirit. My knowledge was increasing, and I was seeking everything God had. I told him I wanted everything. He said, "Okay, when you give Me everything." As I searched to find the truth, I would stay up at night and start studying early mornings and at work. I wanted the peace in the love of Christ because I never knew real love before Jesus and now understand there is a God. I also learned God wants us to find His knowledge and love in His words. That is why, in Second Peter, chapter 1, verse 14, it says that He has given us all things pertaining to life and godliness through the knowledge of Him. He has called us to glory and virtue. As I studied, I realized I know all things and have all things, by that I mean what God wants for me in my life.

August 21, 1991, I surrendered and told *God*, "If You are real, show me." He took me back to Vietnam, December 16, 1966, and I went through the whole night that I had died with angels present and a voice that told them to take me back; "I am not finished with him." Then I knew, without a doubt, this is *God*. I said, "*God*, I will surrender everything anytime, anywhere." I felt love I had never known and had the peace that passes all understanding. I soon realized our eyes are the eye gates to the soul. Our ears are the ear gates to our soul. So when we hear ungodly language, we are influenced by what we see and hear. When exposed to TV and social media, we become angry, fearful, we lose patience, become irritated, depressed, and sad. When we go against God's desires, we lose our empathy for others who are hurting. We wonder why we do not have the peace God freely gives to us; it is because we do not seek *Him* daily.

I now have the love that God gave me. I thought, *If I am going to serve God, I need to know the truth.* As I studied, I found out that God is pure love. I found out that He does not want us to hurt, worry, be confused, angry, or sick. *God* gave me His perfect love and healed me. It was like, "If it does not stop, I will die." But it did not matter. I had so much love for people that I had planned to kill. I started to pray with love. And it scared me. I started to search and went to Trinity School of Theology. I graduated and decided I did not want religion; I wanted Jesus. That is when I decided to get a higher education. I went to the University of the Holy Spirit of theology. Second Peter, chapter 1, verses 3 and 4 says that according to his divine power, He has given us all things pertaining to life and Godliness through the knowledge of him that has called us to glory and virtue—meaning glory is presence, virtue, self-generating, and unlimited. How impressive it is to be given everything. If you love Him, He has given you everything. Study the Word, and you will have an understanding of His word and His spirit. First John, chapter 2, verses 20 through 27 says that we have an unction, a deep down rubbed in anointing of the Holy Spirit, and we know all things. I did not understand that, and I was afraid to speak it. I understood, as I read, God was saying that when I surrendered, His spirit and mine became one. He is living in me. And as I needed it, I would have it. *God* does not want us to know things before we are ready to understand.

Jeremiah, chapter 29, verse 11 says, "For I know the plans I have for you, declares the Lord, plans for welfare and not for evil to give you a future and a hope."

# Chapter 4

I read the word every day as we all should, not just read it but study it. This keeps us grounded in *His* love so we do not fall back into our old habits and way of life. We are grounded in God's word. The terrible things in our life will have no place. When we study, we no longer want to watch the terrible things on TV or think about the sad things in our life. Our language changes. Our thoughts change, and we become more in tune to what God wants for our life. We obtain our peace and understanding through the Lord's word. We stop judging, lying, stop committing adultery, fornication, and are convicted by the Holy Spirit to lead a righteous life.

It is important for us to read and study the word so we know the difference between God's word and false doctrine. A lot of new Christians are gullible to what they hear, especially when false doctrine is preached. They do not have the right news. The gospel is the good news. I have the good news that tells me all I need to know. Second Peter, chapter 1, verses 1 through 3, says that He has given us all things pertaining to life and godliness through the knowledge of Him.

All things include our life and what God has given us. The Father, Son, and Holy Spirit which ministers to us and gives us unlimited and never-ending power. The Greek word *yada* means to know, indicates a combination of close, warm, and even passionate intimacy. It produces an edge in a person's life that enables him to trust God and at the same time perceive what he is doing. Care and receive instructions. To be filled, diligent and have a closer relationship than with our spouse. Receive discipline. It produces an edge in a person's life that enables him to trust God and, at the same time, perceive what *he* is doing.

Our sin is all the same because God says sin is sin. We think our sin is not as bad as others. In the past, people with prejudice minds would label others different because of their sexual orientation. They were called not nice names. They would teach the young people that gay people were horrible if they were gay or lesbian. Romans, chapter 2, verse 1 says that if we judge others, we're condemning ourselves. Then I realized, we cannot keep them out of church. They need God, just like everybody else.

In Canada, I preached about same-sex attraction, and the pastor told me, a member of the congregation was gay. You could have your truck taken, plus six months in jail. Because in Canada, you cannot teach on same-sex attraction. I said, "Who cares? I can preach in jail." Henry walked up. I was expecting him to cuss at me, but that was the first time. He said, "That is the first I have heard anyone preach love about *God* loving gays. Thank you for being honest and telling us, there is no difference socially between us." God has blessed me by using my mistakes to help others. It may sound strange, but I thank God for allowing me to reach out to others and to lift others up. God is all inclusive and has shown me how to help others in these situations.

God has allowed me to be a part of his work, to teach of His promises, and to help growing Christians who might make the same mistakes I have. Teach them how much *God* loves them no matter what they have done. AA is a spiritual program taught from the Bible. I was saved from all I had done, and God used AA when He brought me into His plans. He gave me revelations of His love. To let me know He did that, He sent me to the cold Arctic area to save lives for Him. God wants us to prosper and be blessed. *God* used His anointing to prepare me to go minister in places like Attawapiskat and Wemindji in Quebec, Canada, in the Saint James Bay Area. An elder from the churches in Canada sent me to Tennessee to preach at a small church in Cleveland, Tennessee. God allowed me to get connected to the Church of God to assist in building Churches in Canada.

God has blessed me so much by putting me in contact with the men from Tennessee and Canada. When God sent me to the Aboriginals in Canada, I was kept safe and blessed by Him, allowing me to help Pastor Ernie build and repair churches. Even though I am getting old, He brought me through the freezing weather and allowed me to build a fellowship with the natives. I met a native who introduced me to the grand chief; it was an honor. At the time I was there, God also used the natives to open many doors in Ontario and Quebec. The people of the Aboriginal tribes blessed me. They had become my family. They would provide me with my own house, and I could be alone to pray and worship God, study the Bible, and soak in God's presence, giving me people to see and phone numbers to call. Many times, we are so blessed and protected by God that we forget to give thanks to Him for everyday things. One time, my wife and I were taking the youth on a mission trip to a full gospel at the Aboriginal church. As we headed home, the church bus caught on fire. After we put the fire out, we were blessed to have our youth pastor with us, who knew to pray a great and powerful prayer. We asked *God* to rebuke any curses that were spoken against our youth group. We asked *God* to send the curse back to the place of origin. We made it home with no more problems. He said he thought someone had spoken a curse on us because we entered the village of new post against the will of the shaman. They arrived at home the next day, and the Aboriginal pastor called and told us the shamans' sweat tent burned down. After we left, our prayers had been answered. I had kept in touch and made many trips to Canada for years.

I could see them when I started to minister Northern Canada. It was very cold; it was negative forty-seven degrees in April. I loved Canada, and I loved the people. The Aboriginals became my family. When I was with them, they would provide me with housing, and I could be alone to pray, worship, and study the Bible and soak in God's presence. Sometimes I would need an interpreter when I would teach *God*'s word to the Inuits (Eskimos).

## China trip

In the church we were attending, New Life Christian fellowship, we were blessed having our new pastor come in. His name was Bob. He took a group of us to China for a vacation. we used the vacation time to minister while we could. We didn't go as a church group; we went as tourist. It was a different atmosphere, and this situation was very different. We went to a place called Silk Alley. We met a lot of people there. We tried to get in touch with the deaf so my wife and I could minister to them. We tried with the tourist guides, taxi drivers, and anyone we could talk to, but there were no deaf in Beijing. We went to the Tiananmen Square. We went all over Beijing. We even went to McDonald's. My wife had asked for iced tea, and they gave her ice cream. But that was okay; we like ice cream.

One day, we were walking downtown with the pastor. As we walked, a young man came up and handed the pastor some CDs. These were illegal to have. The pastor looked at me, and he said to look to our left as the police were follow-ing us. Then he asked me, "You're holding those C's for me. What are you going to do when they come over and ask you what you're doing with those?

I said, "I'll just explain to them. I'm carrying them for the pastor."

He gave me a surprised look. As we walked, we got into Tiananmen Square. People were lining up near us, trying to get a picture and not letting us know they were getting it. So we offered to stand with them, and they took a lot of pictures of us. Later, we went back to the hotel we were staying in that evening. We went to bed, and then in the morning when we woke up, we knew we had tried everything to find some deaf to sign with. So we asked *God* to send us some deaf people. "We can't find the deaf, but we're not giving up. Only You can provide them for us to minister to."

At that time, the phone rang. It was Pastor Bob. He said, "Tell Diane we have four deaf persons in the lobby."

Diane replied, "What? He thinks this is funny? Let's go downstairs and see what's going on."

We went down. And as the elevator opened, we saw a group of deaf people sitting at the table. There were workers around them that were going to kick them out of the hotel because it was a five-star hotel. Diane walked up to the table and started to sign to them. They got up and turned to bow to her. They didn't know her. I asked her, "What are they saying?"

She said, "You can see what they're saying," but I couldn't understand it. She was signing in Chinese sign lan-guage, so I just sat there and watched. The Holy Spirit used her to sign. There was a table next to us with a group of missionaries from Wisconsin. One of them walked over to the table and explained that they were teaching English at the University of Beijing. They asked if they could meet the deaf we were talking with. They had been trying to meet with them. They had been praying for six years, trying to meet the deaf. Diane said yes. So they met. They explained to one of them they could speak Mandarin fluently. She started talking to the young girl with them. As they talked, they found out the older lady had been a Christian since 1948. Then they explained to us that we had been invited to their house, which was an underground church, for dinner. We graciously accepted. We had finally been put in contact with the deaf. From there, we were invited to lunch. And when we arrived at the restaurant, we found about five tables full of deaf people. One of the girls, they called her Dimples. And one of the guys, they called Butterfly because he had big ears. They brought a fish out in a big plastic bag, and they asked Diane if that was okay. Diane said yes, and she asked God to make sure it was cooked when they brought it out. The restaurant we ate in is the same one that the president ate at when he came over. We knew it was expensive, but Dimples said she was buying our dinner.

We went back to the hotel that morning. As we were getting ready to leave and go back home, a lot of the deaf showed up with gifts. We had to buy some suitcases to bring them home in. Diane and Dimples exchanged addresses. She wanted Diane to sponsor her to come to the states. But after about three months of corresponding with each other, it seemed to stop. We found out the police had raided the church. We received a picture of temples in Italy. We found out she owned a big business, making clothing. After that, we hardly ever heard from them. We would get a card from them or a letter and would take it down to a Chinese restaurant to have one of the ladies interpret for us. Then she would write back to help us communicate. We went to an orphanage north of Beijing, and we met some children. One had a birth defect, and I tried to pick him up, but he wouldn't come to me So I picked him up anyway. He was resisting. But actually, after a little bit, he cuddled up to me. As we were getting ready to leave, he wouldn't let go of me. I still remember how he hung on to me, and I'll always remember.

When the pastor and I were walking around the market, we walked over to a stand, selling sandwiches. All of a sudden, the little girls came out from underneath the stand and was looking up, holding their hands up, saying something. Pastor said, "I think they're hungry." He bought some food and gave it to them to eat. They acted like they had never eaten. When we see things like that, we know how blessed we are. We were invited to a disco with the deaf. That's how they enjoyed music; they could feel the vibrations. We didn't go with them because we were afraid to be seen with them too much. The police would think something, so we stayed home and went back to the hotel and wrapped our gifts they had given us.

We spent the evening thinking about how much *God* had blessed us when we think about where we came from to where God had taken us. It's awesome. But then we know we are a new creature (Corinthians 5:17). One of the best parts of this trip is, I got to have most of the sushi. We had Sister Bonnie Croft with us. She went with Diane to the Beijing shopping center. Bonnie had never been in the Orient and didn't know their customs. We went through a different part of Beijing, and we saw a lot of people being beaten on. When we got back to the hotel, we started packing to go home. That was the sad part but knew we were very blessed to have been on this trip.

Since we came back, there's been a lot of things that happened. My granddaughter Jade has completed her master's degree and is looking for a good job. Bailey has started playing soccer again and is hoping to go professional. My son Michael has been a big blessing. We're hoping to go down and visit him. My son John passed away. But just before he went or God took him, he called me. He said, "Dad, you don't have to worry about me and God. I'm right with Him, and I'm praying a lot." Sometimes, we don't know what's going to happen. But if we leave it in God's hands, it turns out perfect. I praise God for all He's done in my life. And sometimes I think, *Isn't God awesome?* He has been in my life, and I wouldn't change a thing. I have the best.

I was blessed to meet some Chinese in the town of Longlac, Canada, my friends. We were very blessed by different companies. They would get doors and windows free or at a percentage of the cost. Big Lots blessed the Aboriginals in Canada with pairs of gloves, shoes, clothing, and many other items. I transported these items to the subarctic for the families in need. The pastor at the church in Moosonee needed some young people. It was hard to get them to come on Sunday mornings. I brought some big bags of candy from Sam's Club to take back to Canada with me. I checked the large bags of candy and filled my arctic coat pockets. It held almost a bag in both pockets. I walked down the street to a store on Saturday night called Necessities.

There were some youngsters outside, trying to play hockey. So I pulled out some Tootsie Rolls. I opened one up, let them see me eat it. I pulled some more out and asked if they wanted some. And with a big smile, they said yes. One of them asked if he could have one for his cousin or friend. I knew we had Ernie's problem solved. I asked the group of kids if they would come to church on Sunday at the Aboriginal church, and I would give them some more candy if they came. As I went into church, Ernie said, "I have a problem. We have so many kids here. The upstairs is full, in both rooms, and now they are in the kitchen."

I smiled and said, "Well, your youth problem is solved."

I was able to see how *God* would heal people, cast out demons, how blind eyes see again, legs healed from infirmities. *God* was using young people to heal arthritic hands so twisted that they could not open everyday items without help. Instantly, some were slain in the Spirit because the glory of *God* was present. I never give the credit to the people; *God* gets all the glory. *God* uses us to do what He needs to be done. *God* has given me a mission to preach the gospel in Canada, to lead the lost and suffering into *His* kingdom. I was obedient to listen to the Lord. So when my time had come to start a new ministry, I was a little sad, yet I know this is God's plan. I will do as *He* sees fit and not follow my own instructions. I always knew that the person did not do it. It was God who used us to do what He wanted to get done. God said, "I sent you to Canada to preach the gospel, to bring in the last in the suffering. You have done that. You have seen Me (*God*) do miracles." And I have been obedient. Maybe that is why my ministry changed. I really missed the Aboriginals, and I really love God. He is sending me to a better ministry, helping with the end-time church of dry bones from the streets and recovering addicts.

God is blessing me and using me for ministries that others do not have a testimony to use. God said to me, "Only use the Bible. Share your experiences about drugs and other social issues and afflictions. I have given you a ministry that you can draw on your own experiences in. Doctors can only do so much."

We need to realize God is in control. He uses the low to show His mercies and grace. We can help others if we will give God all. I did that on August 21, 1991, and that is my born-again and my natural birthday.

> And I heard the man clothed in
> linen, which was upon the waters of the

river. When he held up his right hand and his left hand unto heaven, and swear by him that live forever, that it shall be for a time, times, and a half, and when we shall have accomplished to scatter the power of the holy people, all these things shall be finished.

And I heard but I understood not then said I, Oh my Lord, what shall be the end of these things?

And he said, go thy way, Daniel, for the words are closed up and sealed till the end of time.

Many shall be purified, made white, and tried, but the wicked shall do wickedly and none of the wicked shall understand. (Daniel 12:7–10)

But the wise shall understand. And *God* said, "Those who do know their *God* will be strong and do exploits." And then I knew that's what *God* was doing with me. To know *God* is to know *Him* more intimately than my wife. And I do know my Father in heaven that way. Now I am feeling led to witness and teach people who are addicted to alcohol and drugs and to teach on the end-times and dry bones. God is blessing and using me for ministries that others do not want or feel led to address, the social issues that are a hot topic. I am being used to help addicts through *God's* word. Doctors can only do so much, but *God* can do everything. He is in control. He uses the low to show His mercies and grace. We can all help others if we will give *God* all. I did that on August 21, 1991. That is my natural birthday. That is the day I gave my heart to the Lord. I think, if *God* can use me, a sinner, *He* can use anyone.

Being available to study and read the word, sorting out things, and spreading the good news is what *God* has placed me here for. *God* has opened many doors for me. I believe my obedience to *Him* has allowed Him to bless me and my family.

We know *God* when we talked to Him all day long as being beside us. Sometimes, when I sit around and start praying, people look at me like I have lost my mind. One time I had a spirit of confusion on me, and I was saying things that were not true and tried to make them believe it. I instantly asked Jesus to rebuke it, and it was gone. As I continued to teach, the congregation was shocked at what *God* had done for me. This is normal to me because I know that *God* does everything for me when I obey *Him*, and I learned that from being obedient. When God tells me to go, I go because He has opened many doors for me.

Witnessing has to go beyond words. Our actions are also an important vehicle for demonstrating our faith in the impact of knowing and loving God and knowing that we are loved by God has on our lives. First Peter chapter 3, verse 15 says, "But in your hearts revere Christ Lord." Proverbs, chapter 10, verse 22, says that it is the blessing of the Lord that makes rich and adds no sorrow to it. The foundation for wealth and prosperity is God's blessing. Genesis chapter 13, verse 2, says, Abraham was extraordinarily rich in livestock and silver because God's blessing was upon him, and he exceled in all he did. There is always an inner peace that accompanies financial blessings that comes from God. In essence, money is not evil but the love of it. Also, it is God's blessings that guarantee long-lasting wealth and prosperity.

# Chapter 5

## Prosperity teachings

A lot of people think the big churches are a moneymaking venture. I found myself using the same thought pattern. I started to wonder why all this money for God's kingdom is being used for a bigger house, bigger airplane. I heard one preacher say, "I want a thoroughbred." God wants to bless His anointed, and it is not for me to say who and how God blesses them with substantial amounts of money, property, or other blessings God decides to bless someone with. Because of hate and confusion that we experience with our family members, they are being put in shackles and expected to be poor if they choose to be a pastor or religious leader. God provides all and blesses them in all sorts of ways. Now I realized, I had had the same problems and thought behaviors with certain stars and singers and other wealthy people. God revealed to me. I believe He said, "Think about this, and you will know I am God. I give and take away as I see fit. It is not for you to judge, only Me."

Pastors that have large congregations, I thought, are living extravagant lifestyles. They have jets, nice homes, and airports large enough to land four jets. My thoughts were that some are used as a moneymaking scheme. I would get into arguments about pastors receiving millions of dollars. I realized my thought process was not God's process. God wants to bless His elders and His saints and all of the people that are bringing forth His word. He does this in the way he sees fit and not how I view things. I thank God for His wisdom and calling pastors who do not preach on hellfire and damnation and for teaching on God's promises and His love for us. Some pastors teach false doctrines. Some offend people. And some drive people away with their teaching. God has revealed to me that He reaches all people in diverse ways. He can see what they need and lead them in His ways. I have found the truth in the word and hope others will seek Him and surrender their lives according to His word and love. I also feel that families attending and seeking *God* need to show by example how their lives have been changed by reading the word at home and seeking *God* publicly and not just when you are in a church service. Our children learn from our example. And when we praise and give *God* thanks in public and show His love in our lives, they are more likely to follow our example.

So many people have been taught and have attended many different denominations. I have observed pastors' different teachings, and then they try to figure out what all of this means. I have found that when I study the word and allow God's Holy Spirit to teach me from His word that I can learn and study a lot more on my own to understand God's desire and plan for my life. I am not suggesting that we ignore our pastor's word or his thoughts on the word. I am just saying that as an individual, I take it seriously to study the word on my own and allow the Holy Spirit to guide and direct to me. It is particularly important that we are a witness of Jesus and God the Father to other people who may need His love. I try not to judge people on what I have heard them say or have seen them do.

Sometimes we ask, "Why are all these things happening to me?" When we apply the word in our lives, we need to have compassion and empathy enough to see a change in our own lives, as well as in others. If we study the word, Jesus is the word. We would be more like Jesus wants us to be, all the same minds. Then we listen to the old falseness in some old doctrines that have been taught wrong. And they cannot be found in the Bible. Some preachers are illiterate, or this is hard for them to understand. Some have been lured away by some man who has preached. Some pastors do not have an intimate relationship with God but the church and religion. God speaks and warns us not to do what man teaches to follow God's word only. The Holy Ghost can teach us and lead us. He teaches us through revelation and dreams. According to 1 John 2:27, "But you have received the Holy Spirit, and He lives within you, so you do not need anyone to teach you what is true." We need to confirm God's word. In John, chapter 2, verse 20 through 27, it tells us we know all things spiritually. When we are born again, God's spirit is joined with ours, and He knows all things. And if you have a fellowship with Him, He is our source, kind of like a computer, only better and faster. When we listen to God and study His word, we know the truth when we hear the word and have studied and meditated on it. God knows when a preacher is making a statement about the word. And we may know that it is instantly wrong. Do not get angry or upset because we may have listened to one of the preachers who did not know, so do not be upset with him. God does not reveal everything at the same time. God uses His pastors, preachers, priests, and other holy men, but we need to be careful. Do not do or say things before we say what we think because the Lord may say, "Hey, go read My word to show yourself approved."

*God* wants to live in our lives, and He also wants us to be happy. His perfect love surrounds us, and all we need do is surrender and keep a close relationship to Father in prayer. It also gives you peace that passes all understanding. I find this to be true because God shows me in diverse ways. I felt the anointing of God and was bold and talking about Jesus. I was excited. I knew God had sent me there to witness to other patients. My wife said, "I do not understand why you go out of your way to witness."

I replied, "God gives me boldness. And today I go out of my way to be the very bold and best God wants me to be." God wants me to show people His love and for them to surrender their lives to Jesus. I believe, if more people will go out of their way to be bold, we will see a revival. I know God is helping me to write this. Almost everything I am writing, I do not remember and would never put it together like I have. I am starting to have doors open, and I know God has prepared me to teach. Do not call me a pastor because I am my teacher. I can relate to other people in a way because of the anointing that I have experienced. I am not Pastor Benny or David Hogan. I do not even put myself in that class. I am just hitting the beginning because there is no way I could be as spiritual as people think without God using me. I have friends who refer to me as a saint because it is no longer I who live but Jesus who lives in me. He gets all the glory.

I get phone calls. I am jokingly called Saint Lawrence of Byronia. There are people of different religions and backgrounds. They know I read the Bible and study the word. There was a lady I know who asked me if our church would put a petition before *God* to keep her son and his fellow soldiers safe. I had asked her later how her son was doing. She excitedly replied, "Nobody in his unit was hurt, and all praise is given to God for His protection." She also said that no group that size has ever been through that experience with so few casualties, unless they were in administration. Some had been shot, but all had survived. I know God was protecting them because of the petition we put in front of God. He hears our prayers and is faithful to answer. When we show God's love to other people, there is no limit to what God can do in their lives. People look to us for help, and we are supposed to cry out to God for them. Praying for our families and our children, who are being influenced by society, is so important that we should seek their protection from God.

> For the word of God is quick and powerful and sharper than any two-edged sword, piercing even to the dividing asunder of soul and spirit of the joints and marrow. And it is a discerner of the thoughts and intents of the heart. (Hebrews 4:12)

> Study to show thyself approved unto God, a Workman that needed not to be ashamed, rightly dividing the word of truth. (2 Timothy 2:15)

> And the servant of the Lord must not strive, but be gentle unto all men, apt to teach, patient. (2 Timothy 2:24)

> Now these Jews were no more noble than those in Thessalonica. They received the word with all eagerness, examining the scriptures daily to see if these things were so. (Acts 17:11)

> Then shall I not be ashamed when I have respect unto all thy commandments?

I will praise thee with uprightness of
heart when I shall have learned thy righteous judgments. (Psalm 119:6–7)

A new commandment I give to
you that you love one another, just as I
have loved you. You Also are to love one
another. (John 13:34)

Beloved, if God so loved us, we all
also ought to love one another. (1 John
4:11)

Hatred stirs up strife, but love cov-
ers all offenses. (Proverbs 10:12)

Owe no one anything except to love
each other for the one who loves another,
has fulfilled the law. (Romans 13: 18)

I' m going to try to explain what has transpired and
how God is using me as an instrument. When I started to
draft this book, I knew I had no experience in writing. I also
knew that I had the anointing to write because God was giving me this word. I remember, when I was first born again,
I began to fast and pray for three days, seven days, ten days,
thirty days. I even fasted forty days with the help of my doctor. My fasting continued in diverse ways and times. I tried
to regularly fast, and this continued for a long time. I was
diagnosed with A1C type 1 diabetes and high blood pressure.
The last few months, I lost about eighty pounds. And a few
months ago, my doctor said my Trulicity was working a little
too well. My A1C dropped from 7.3 to 5.6, so my dose was

lowered and then discontinued. I have been able to maintain good health.

My doctor said, "I have seen miracles before," just like my diabetes. But I knew my blood pressure was still a little high. My diabetes is under control through God. I am seventy-seven years old. I was supposed to die, according to my doctor, thirty years ago. I have been healed and have a peace and faith that surpasses all understanding. My health is better than ever So I have made a commitment to exercise and work out daily. If I remember, my memory is being evaluated. I am seeing a neurologist, and he said, I may have a little dementia. But he cannot tell me that I do not know God or remember what God said about my health. God cured me and restored my body and mind and all things. I have given you all things pertaining to life and righteousness. Theologians who studied this should realize, God said that He can cure you and save you. As I read the Bible, I realize, God fills us with His anointing and fills us like an ink pen. He can use people to write what He wants us to know. This is why I know God gave me the words for this book. God and I have collaborated on this work. If I have offended God or written something wrong, I ask that He forgive me.

I know I am far from perfect. But when I was first saved, I thought I was perfect and pure. I know I still have prejudice left in me. God showed me this through an incident, and I woke up to the facts one night when I arrived home. My wife said, "Your daughter has something to tell you." So I went up to her room and asked, "What do you have to tell me?"

She was crying and said, "I cannot tell you."

Then I got angry and said, "You have to tell me."

She said, "I am pregnant."

I became angry and thought, *I am a Christian, and my daughter is pregnant.* Then she really blew up my religious mind and told me the father was Black. I lost it and realized I still had prejudicial thoughts. I asked God why, and I started to remember all my life. I had those thoughts beat into me, almost seven years in the military, indoctrinated by what I had seen and heard.

I had a tough time with anger, fear, depression, and stayed alone with God to help me cope with the situation.

Two of my best friends, Terry and Nick, came alongside to help me. We started a prayer room, and Terry told me a story about a woman. She had a daughter with a boyfriend who was not nice. The mother told her she should leave him, but her daughter married him anyway. After a couple of years, she had two daughters. The grandmother was babysitting for her grandchildren when the pastor showed up and asked, "Wouldn't it be nice if I were God and could turn back the hands of time, and your daughter had never met her boyfriend? You would not have to worry anymore."

She answered, "Yes."

Then the pastor said, "You know what I would do next?"

And she said, "What?"

"I would go in the kitchen, take the girls away from the mother."

Then the mother said, "Wait."

The pastor said, "If your daughter never met him, she would not have them."

She started to cry and said, "No, I do not want to change anything."

That changed my heart, and I realized how blessed I am to have my grandsons. I never want to change anything in my life that God has given me.

> Have I not commanded you? Be
> strong and courageous. Do not be fright-
> ened and do not be dismayed for the

Lord your God is with you wherever you go. (Joshua 1:9)

For I know the plans I have for you, declares the Lord, plans for welfare and not for evil to give you a future and a hope. (Jeremiah 29:11)

I appeal to you, therefore, brothers, by the mercies of God, to be present in your bodies as a living sacrifice, holy and acceptable to God, which is your spiritual worship, do not be conformed to this world, but be transformed by the renewal of your mind, that by testing you may discern what is the will of God, what is good and acceptable and perfect. (Romans 12:1–2)

Therefore, if anyone is in Christ, he is a new creation. The old has passed away. Behold the new has come. (2 Corinthians 5:17)

For the scripture reads, whosoever believeth on him shall not be ashamed. For there is no difference between the Jew and the Greek for the same Lord over all is rich unto all that call upon him. (Romans 10:11–12)

There is neither Jew nor Gentile, neither slave nor free. Nor is there male

and female, for you are all one in Christ
Jesus. (Galatians 3:28)

I became fired up for God as a young Christian. I prayed
and fasted. I had intimate sessions with God and thought I
am so sold out to God; I could see no wrong in my life. I
asked people, "If you see or hear me do or say anything, tell
me. I do not want to do anything to displease God." I even
asked God to show me if there was anything displeasing, and
I found out God is not politically correct when He talks to
us.

I started to think, *Why me, Lord.*

The Lord said to me, "You are prejudice, and most of
your service friends are, but your father was not."

I thought, *Then why am I?* I realized I had been taught
not to be prejudice. But when I heard it was my daughter, I
had angry thoughts. If I had waited to respond to things, it
would have been a different outcome. I know it is not godly
to have those type of prejudicial thoughts. Also, when I was
upset for three or four months, I realized I was the one who
suffered by allowing it to continue. Sometimes we have to
accept our situations and allow God to change our thought
process.

After I had learned of my daughter's pregnancy, I went
back to Canada to see my friend Ernie to relax and get away
from the depression I felt about my daughter and my new
Black grandson. I started to feel better. So I returned home,
and my wife informed me the baby was to be born in a few
weeks. I said, "Okay, we can go to visit her and the baby once
she had given birth. He would be named Cameron. I will
stay about fifteen to twenty minutes so she would not feel
bad because we did come up to visit her."

Man, God surprised me by giving me a love so strong
for my new grandson. When I looked at him, he was an olive

color, like Jesus, and I started to cry. I said, "God, you have given me a little piece of Jesus." And I realized, only God could break my prejudices by giving me a love for my new grandson. It was about eight hours later when my wife said his other grandparents and family were waiting outside to see him. I said, "Okay, they can come in."

My wife, Diane, said, "Larry, the other family have been waiting and want to see him. We get to bring him home, and he can stay with us."

I may have said, "We can come back to see him after they leave," but it was hard to leave the room. God had placed so much love inside me for this little piece of heaven. I began to take him shopping with me to Kroger's to show him off to the ladies. Some would ask, "Is he your son?"

I said, "No, he is my grandson."

On the way, sometimes he would reach his small hand over and touch mine and say, "I love you, Papa," and I would look back to the road and feel tears running down my face.

He stayed with us until she met her husband, Bill. They moved into their own home and planned their wedding. My friend Terry even went overboard and cooked dinner for the wedding. I knew he had spent his own money to buy stuff for the dinner. So when I think about it, I get choked up. We spent a lot of time with Cameron. I helped Cameron build a four-by-six shed with pallets. Cameron had wanted to build one because he had watched his uncle John build one and had remembered the experience. Later, they moved to Texas. They bought a house near a Dallas Cowboys player. Cameron enjoyed football. I thought, *How impressive. God had placed them near a Dallas Cowboys player.*

When they would come home from Texas, he would run right to me. I would tell him, "We need to use your time wisely because you are going home in two weeks."

He would say, "I am home" and would run off, so I would be unable to say anything.

We were later blessed with having an adopted grandson, my daughter's stepson, and also two more grandsons. We are still a close and loving family. People ask, "What happened for you to have such a nice family?" So I tell them God blessed us. He never makes mistakes. I thank God for my sons-in-law.

One day at church, my friend Bonnie approached us. She said Bill wanted to accept Jesus as his Savior. I was blessed to be asked to pray with him. I got so nervous; Bonnie had to finish it for me. I do not have enough time to write about all eleven grandchildren, but I cherish them all equally. It has been so exciting as each one becomes older to see their personalities come out. It is hard to believe sometimes that God has blessed me with such a loving family.

BJ is my grandson. He knows the Bible and excels at everything. He has the wisdom to give up the things he loves if it is not pleasing to God. Courtney is a real blessing. We were close. He is as close to me as my biological grandsons. I love him. And when he calls me Grandpa, it warms my heart.

Brandon is also special to us. When he lived with us, he would fold his clothes on his bed without being asked. He would follow me around as I was fishing. Brandon was late to school one day, and the principal was angry because he was late. He told the principal, "Grandpa made me have a Bible study. That is why I was late." Brandon is the kind of person that loves people. He never leaves a friend behind. When he comes to see all of his old friends, their parents love to have him come stay the night, and even on some weekends.

We wonder why there is discrimination between the races while, surprise, God created us all the same. We have a behavior problem that does not come from the color of our skin. I have mixed grandsons, and I love them with a godly love. We need to love all people. And we can accomplish this with God's love. We talk about prejudice. All people have it in one form or another. I am seeing less and less though, as people seek God. And this is a good thing. Because of the changes I have seen in my lifetime, humanity is still striving to make changes. There is a lot more to be done. I see families in diverse groups respond to my grandsons positively. I really get excited when I see different races coming together in a positive manner. I have a spirit of God in me. I have no fear or worries because the Bible says that perfect love casts out all fear. God also says to not worry or to be confused about His love, and I have that perfect love God has given to me. I value and respect all of God's creations. I know God loves us all and wants us to have the same mind. We can have all those things when we surrender our lives to Jesus.

> For as many of you as were baptized into Christ, have put on Christ. There is neither Jew nor Greek. There is neither slave nor free. There is no male and female, for you are all one in Christ Jesus. And if you are Christ, then you are Abraham's offspring. Heirs according to promise. (Galatians 3:27–29)

Diana Joe, my granddaughter, is the light of my life. I am blessed to have her in my life. My grandson Garrett was premature. He only weighed one pound, fourteen ounces. The doctor said we needed to let him go, but Grandma Diane said, "No way. I serve an impressive God." We prayed, and he started to drop weight. He dropped to only fifteen ounces, so she said, "I will pray more." And when she would hold him, his oxygen level would go up, and he graduated with honors.

Hunter is a bright spot in our lives. He has been a blessing to us and his parents. My wife thinks, since we have the most loving family, we need to write about the miracles we have seen.

Nick was my sports nut. He set a lot of school and state records and was invited to breakfast at Michigan State. They wanted to offer him a scholarship, but he wound up boxing in the UFC. He never lost a fight. But he stopped because he told me, "Grandpa, I do not want to hurt anyone." He had a big heart and would come over, and we would play together. About a week to ten days before Nick passed away, he told me boldly, "Hey, I am right with Jesus."

Jade and Bailey are both very athletic and incredibly beautiful. They excel in soccer. I have enough to draft a book on each one, but that is for another time.

# Chapter 6

When I was fired up about God as a young Christian, I prayed, fasted, and had intimate sessions with God. I thought I am so sold out to God there could be nothing wrong with my life. I would ask people, "If you see or hear me do or say anything, tell me." I ask God to show me if there is anything displeasing. I found out God is not politically correct when He talks to us. God does not have to worry about being politically correct because he is all-knowing. If we take time with the Lord, He will bless us with more than we could ever ask for. Sometimes we have to accept our situations and allow *God* to change our thought process in order for us to live a better life.

Our church and many other churches in Michigan and in other states are seeing people in hospitals and other facilities being healed and God moving in diverse ways in their lives. I have seen God do works in my own family. Before our pastor had moved into the missions field, God had blessed my wife, Diane, by having people coming to ask for her to pray for them. She had been given a boldness to take their requests to the Lord in prayer. I get excited to see the changes that the Lord has seen to do in my family. I have seen many people healed and surrender their lives to the love and grace of *God.* It is like God explained to me during in my last ministry of preaching and said, "The anointing I give you is mine, and the anointing I give is like an ink pen. When you put ink into an ink pen, it writes and needs to be refilled." So when I feel tapped out, *God* refills me with His Holy Spirit. In the same way, when I was at a low point in my life, *God* would direct me home to rest and be refilled with His spirit. We all need time to rest. It is a physical need everyone has. It took me a while to understand that I could not be effective in ministry when I deplete my physical self. I would find myself so excited about *God's* message and wanting to share it every day with everyone. I exhausted myself and was not achieving what *God* had planned for my life. Some people have asked me, "How do you find time to study and read the word, sorting everything out?" I tell them I do not, but I thank God used me as a secretary to write what He wants. I thought that if God can use a sinner like me, He can use anyone So I thought, *Why can't I give myself a secretary?* So God sent my niece over to help me out. I know she is the one God sent because she is a recovered alcoholic and prescription drug abuser. God has restored her soul and spirit.

I have seen her being used by God in diverse ways, such as caring for her mother who suffered from Alzheimer's and dementia. She had given nine years to the care and everyday needs of her mother. I saw the determination and faith she had to follow *God's* plan instead of her own. After her mother (my sister) had passed, she found herself homeless as the house she was to inherit did not come to a reality. She remained steadfast, and *God* blessed her by giving her a place to live with her daughter and son-in-law. They had given her a private part of the home to live in and the extra blessing of being able to watch her grandchildren on a daily basis. I enjoy having her over to type in my book with an added bonus of sharing my testimony and watching how *God* has changed her life. We are all made in *God's* image, and she is a kind soul. I am pretty handsome. Well, I am entitled to my opinion, and we can all dream.

> Create in me a clean heart, O God,
> and renew a right spirit within me.
> (Psalm 55:10)

> And I will give you a new heart and
> a new spirit I will put within you, and
> I will remove the heart of stone from
> your flesh and give you a heart of flesh.
> (Ezekiel 36:26)

> Do not be conformed to this world,
> but be transformed by the renewal of
> your mind, that by testing you may
> discern what is the will of God, what is
> good, acceptable, and perfect. (Romans
> 12:2)

Prescription drug abuse is the fourth highest type of substance abuse after tobacco, alcohol, and marijuana. Alcoholism is defined as the inability to regulate one's drinking as a result of a physical and emotional reliance on alcohol. Alcoholism is a pattern of alcohol abuse that often leaves its victims in bad shape.

> Here is my servant, whom I have
> chosen, the one I love and whom I
> delight. I will put my spirit in him, and
> he will proclaim justice to the nations.
> (Matthew 12:4)

> What man among you? If he has
> one hundred sheep and loses one of
> them, does not leave the ninety-nine in
> the pasture and go after the one that is
> lost until he finds it. (Luke 15:4)

We are like the sheep; we do not have the ability to find our way home. This is why we need Jesus as our shepherd. Just as shepherds would keep their sheep in a safe field, surrounded by stone walls, there's only one place to enter and exit. Jesus keeps us under His protection so that we are able to live productively and to live our full lives.

> My Dear children, I write this to
> you so that you will not sin. But if any-
> one does sin, we have an advocate with
> the Father, Jesus Christ the righteous
> one. He is the atoning sacrifice for our
> sins, not only for our sins, but also for the
> sins of the world. (1 John 2:1–2)

We are given this promise because *God* knew we would be born into sin. No one lives a life without sin. The Father knew we would need an advocate, so *He* gave His only Son so we would be able to have eternal life. Once we surrender and live our lives for Christ, we begin to see changes in our behaviors. This is due to the grace and mercy that *God* has given us through His Son. When we acknowledge that we need the forgiveness and love of Jesus, we can start to become a new creation truly made in His image

> He was given authority, glory and
> sovereign power, all nations and peoples
> of every language worshipped him. His

dominion is an everlasting dominion that will not pass away, and his Kingdom is one that will never be destroyed. (Daniel 7:14)

And my God will supply every need of yours according to his riches in glory and Christ Jesus. (Philippians 4:19)

Every good gift and every perfect gift is from above coming down from the father of lights with whom there is no variation or shadow due to change. (James 1:17)

Give and it will be given to you. Good measure. Press down shaken together. Running over will be put into your lap. For with the measure, you use it, it will be measured back to you. (Luke 6:38)

Fear not, for I am with you. Be not dismayed, for I am your God. I will strengthen you. I will help you. I will uphold you with my righteous right hand. (Isaiah 41:10)

Man is spiritually dead, but God intervenes and makes that man spiritually alive. Without regeneration, there will be no justification or sanctification.

One usage of our English word *anoint* comes from the Greek word *chrio*. It means to consecrate, to set apart, and empower Jesus as the Christ and Messiah. In this instance of the word, Jesus alone is the anointed King.

> But the anointing that you received from him abides in you, and you have no need that anyone should teach you. But as his anointing teaches you about everything and is true and is no lie, just as it has taught you, abide in him. (1 John 2:27)

> The spirit of the Lord is upon me because he has anointed me to proclaim good news to the poor. He has sent me to proclaim liberty to the captives and recovering of sight to the blind, to set at liberty those who are oppressed. (Luke 4:18)

Funny how God works. My sister Jackie invited our daughter, Heather, to church. And she accepted Jesus. Then Heather invited us to church. We got saved. It took a lot for me to surrender. When I went to Dr. Pinwells, He found a lump in my throat and told me to see a doctor about my cancer. I went to an oncologist to see if I had cancer. When he checked it, he said yes. It was my thyroid, and it had spread to my lungs. So I knew then I had to surrender. I said, "Jesus, if you are real, show me," and He did. He took me back to Vietnam when I was pronounced dead, and then that's the time I surrendered. I received more love in that moment than I had ever felt before. And it was like, if I had more love, it would kill me. I didn't care. But sometimes it takes a lot to make us surrender. That's what I'm asking God for to bring my family in. And I know because of the Bible, it will happen. I'm already seeing results. Our children have all came back to God. So I can never stop serving Him. I can never retire. I don't need money.

Sometimes churches will take up a love offering for me. That helps. But my next venture is to go to Bethesda and to teach at a rescue mission. I was hoping they would let me share one of their beds before I got saved. My big thing was money. I wanted more and more. But today, money doesn't mean anything to me. That's because God's taken the desire and need from me. I see you're thinking about all the things about the miracles I have seen God do. I still marvel, but I know it's true. It's hard to please God. But I think I've pleased Him in what He's allowing me to do. I can stay here, looking out my window. I'm so pleased and so content in what God has done. I've met the grand chief, been all over Canada to preach. *He* has allowed me to teach, to evangelize, and have done the work of a prophet. When God allows me to, I would do the work of an apostle. But I don't feel that I am worthy. But thank *You*, Father, that *You* have allowed me to do the work You have placed in my charge.

# About the Author

William Browning was born on August 21, 1944, in Allen Junction, West Virginia. His parents are Roscoe and Lola Browning, coal miner and homemaker.

He is the last child of five siblings. He served in the Air Force during the Vietnam War for six and a half years.

He is married to Diane Browning for fifty-three years, the father of four children, the grandfather of ten children, and the great-grandfather of four children.